D1632375

Weather Lore

Volume III

The Elements

Richard Inwards

Weather Lore

A Collection of
Proverbs, Sayings & Rules
Concerning the Weather

Volume III

The Elements ~
Clouds, Mists, Haze, Dew, Fog,
Rain, Rainbows

Published in Great Britain in 2013 by
Papadakis Publisher

P PAPADAKIS

An imprint of New Architecture Group Limited

Kimber Studio, Winterbourne, Berkshire, RG20 8AN, UK
info@papadakis.net | www.papadakis.net

@papadakisbooks   PapadakisPublisher

Publishing Director: Alexandra Papadakis
Design: Alexandra Papadakis
Editorial Assistant: Juliana Kassianos

First published in 1898 by Elliot Stock, 62 Paternoster Row, London

ISBN 978 1 906506 39 1

Images for this volume were taken from the publications, with the exception of those that were in the public domain:
"Autour De La Lune", "British Birds Vols I & II", "Dictionary of Gardening", "Familiar Wild Flowers", "Le
Grandes Inventions Modernes", "La Lecture en Famille", "Le Livre de la Ferme Vols I & II", "Merveilles de la
Nature", "Les Merveilles du Monde", "Old Farms, Science For All", "The Fruit Growers Guide Vols I, II &
III", "Under the Rainbow Arch", "Universal Instructor Vols I, II & III".

We gratefully acknowledge the permission granted to use these images. Every possible attempt has been
made to identify and contact copyright holders. Any errors or omissions are inadvertent and will be
corrected in subsequent editions.

A CIP catalogue of this book is available from the British Library

Printed and bound in China

Contents

Clouds - An Introduction

As it will be seen, much is to be gleaned by observing the forms and appearances of clouds. By Howard, Fitzroy, and others these masses of vapour have been marshalled in the order of their formation and altitude, so that the most casual observer may soon judge of the age of a cloud, whether seen as a light, filmy cirrus, or in the form of a dark, threatening nimbus, ripe for rain, and spreading like a vampire's wing over the landscape.

Although the names given by Howard to the different clouds have been here adopted, and the same general arrangement maintained, yet the familiar names given to these masses of vapour by sailors and others, such as Mackerel Sky, Mares' Tails, Wool Bags, etc., have not been omitted. Clouds should of course be observed with a proper allowance for the force and direction of the wind at the time. With a swift upper current of air a clear sky sometimes becomes obscured in a few minutes, whilst in calmer weather changes in the appearance of the sky are slow to occur, and can be reckoned on with more safety.

Clouds

And now the mists from earth are clouds in heaven,
Clouds slowly castellating in a calm
Sublimer than a storm, while brighter breathes
O'er the whole firmament the breadth of blue,
Because of that excessive purity
Of all those hanging snow-white palaces:
A gentle contrast, but with power divine.
- Wilson.

While any of the clouds, except the nimbus, retain   Form
their primitive forms, no rain can take place; and it
is by observing the changes and transitions of cloud
form that weather may be predicted.
- Howard.

The higher the clouds, the finer the weather.   High

When on clear days isolated clouds drive over the   Isolated
zenith from the rain-wind side, storm and rain follow
within twenty-four hours.
- United States.

After clouds calm weather.   Calm
- T. Fuller.

Clouds

Dark	Clouds that the sun builds up darken him.
With wind	It will not rain much so long as the sky is clear before the wind; but when clouds fall in against the wind, rain will soon follow.
	When clouds break before the wind, leaving a clear sky, fine weather will follow.
Indications of	After fine, clear weather the first signs in the sky of a coming change are usually light streaks, curls, wisps, or mottled patches of white distant clouds, which increase and are followed by an overcasting of murky vapour that grows into cloudiness. The appearance more or less oily or watery, as wind or rain may prevail, is an infallible sign. Usually the higher and more distant such clouds seem to be, the more gradual, but general, the coming change of weather will prove. - Fitzroy.
Growth of	Now clouds combine, and spread o'er all the sky, When little rugged parts ascend on high, Which may be twined, though by a feeble tie; These make small clouds, which, driven on by wind, To other like and little clouds are joined, And these increase by more: at last they form Thick, heavy clouds; and thence proceeds a storm. - Lucretius (Creech).
Dispersing	When clouds, after rain, disperse during the night, weather will not remain clear.

Can any understand the spreadings of the clouds?
- Job xxxvi. 29.

Dost thou know the balancing of the clouds?
- Job xxxvii. 16.

Bleak is the morn when blows the north from high;
Oft when the dawnlight paints the starry sky,
A misty cloud suspended hovers o'er
Heaven's blessed earth with fertilizing store,
Drained from the living streams: aloft in air
The whirling winds the buoyant vapour bear,
Resolved at eve in rain or gusty cold,
As by the north the troubled rack is rolled.
- Hesiod (Elton).

Clouds without rain in summer indicate wind.
- Theophrastus ("Signs, etc." J. G. Wood's Translation).

Cloudy mornings turn to clear evenings.

When the clouds of the morn to the west fly away,
You may conclude on a settled, fair day.

At sunset with a cloud so black,
A westerly wind you shall not lack.

Many small clouds at north-west in the evening
show that rain is gathering, and will suddenly fall.
- Pointer.

Storm cloud	When a heavy cloud comes up in the south-west, and seems to settle back again, look out for a storm.
Accumulating	If the sky, from being clear, becomes fretted or spotted all over with bunches of clouds, rain will soon fall. - Shepherd of Banbury.
Stationary	When clouds are stationary and others accumulate by them, but the first remain still, it is a sign of a storm. - Theophrastus ("Signs, etc." J. G. Wood's Translation).

Low	If on the ocean's bosom clouds appear, While the blue vault above is bright and clear, These signs by shepherds and by sailors seen, Give pleasing hope of days and nights serene. - Aratus (J. Lamb).
Increasing	If clouds increase visibly, and the clear sky become less, it is a sign of rain.

Like inconstant clouds
That, rack'd upon the carriage of the winds,
Increase.
- Play of King Edward III.
(Sometimes attributed to Shakespeare.)

If the clouds appear to drive fast when there is no
wind, expect wind from that quarter from which they
are driven. But if they gather and collect together,
on the sun's approach to that part, they will begin to
disperse; and then if they disperse towards the north,
it prognosticates wind; if towards the south, rain.
- Bacon.

*Collecting
and driving*

When the carry [current of clouds] gaes west,
Gude weather is past;
When the carry gaes east,
Gude weather comes neist.

Driving

When ye see a cloud rise out of the west,
straightway ye say, There cometh a shower;
and so it is. - Luke xii. 54.

From west

Fear not as much a cloud from the land as from ocean
in winter; but in the summer a cloud from a darkling
coast is a warning.
- Theophrastus ("On Winds" J. G. Wood's Translation).

If the sky clears, and the clouds commence to break
in the quarter opposite the wind, it will be fine; but
if it clear up to windward, it indicates nothing, and
leaves the weather uncertain. - Bacon.

Clearing

Clouds

With mock suns

If clouds shall have shut in the sun, the less light there is left, and the smaller the sun's orb appears, the more severe will the storm prove. But if the disc of the sun appear double or treble, as if there were two or three suns, the storm will be much more violent, and will last many days.
- Bacon.

North-west

If the upper current of clouds comes from the north-west in the morning, a fine day will ensue.

If in the north-west before daylight end there appear a company of small black clouds like flocks of sheep, it is a sure and certain sign of rain.
- Wing, 1649.

If a layer of thin clouds drive up from the north-west, and under other clouds moving more to the south, expect fine weather.
- United States.

In winter and in the North Atlantic a cloud rising from the north-west is an infallible forerunner of a great tempest.
- Kalm ("Travels").

Clouds in the east,
obscuring the sun,
indicate fair weather.

East

In the North Atlantic, if clouds appear during an easterly wind to the south-west, with their points turning to the north-east, it is a sign of a south-west wind in twenty-four hours.
- Kalm (Travels).

If clouds drive up high from the south, expect a thaw.

South

Small scattering clouds flying high in the south-west foreshow whirlwinds.
- Howard.

South-west

A sky covered with clouds need not cause apprehension, if the latter are high, and of no great density, and the air is still, the barometer at the same time being high. Rain falling under such circumstances is generally light, or of not long continuance. - Jenyns.

High

Dark

If high, dark clouds are seen in spring, winter, or fall, expect cold weather.

Dark heavy clouds, carried rapidly along near the earth, are a sign of great disturbance in the atmosphere from conflicting currents. At such times the weather is never settled, and rain extremely probable.
- Jenyns.

Diverging

If the clouds, as they come forward, seem to diverge from a point in the horizon, a wind may be expected from that quarter, or the opposite.
- Thomas Best.

Apparently stationary

The apparent permanency and stationary aspect of a cloud is often an optical deception, arising from the solution of vapour on one side of a given point, while it is precipitated on the other.
- J. F. Daniels.

Against heavy rain every cloud rises bigger than the preceding, and all are in a growing state.
- G. Adams.

Clouds floating low, and casting shadows on the ground, are usually followed by rain.
- United States.

High upper clouds, crossing the sun, moon, or stars in direction different from that of the lower clouds, or the wind then felt below, foretell a change of wind toward their direction.
- Fitzroy.

When the generality of the clouds rack or drive with the wind (though there are many in little fleeces, or long strakes lying higher, and appearing not to move), the wind is flagging, and will quickly change and shift its point. - Pointer.

Clouds

If two strata of clouds appear in hot weather to move in different directions, they indicate thunder.

If, during dry weather, two layers of clouds appear moving in opposite directions, rain will follow.

Clouds floating at different heights show different currents of air, and the upper one generally prevails. If this is north-east, fine weather may be expected; if south-west, rain.
- C. L. Prince.

Cross wind

If you see clouds going across the wind, there is a storm in the air.

If clouds float at different heights and rates, but generally in opposite directions, expect heavy rains.

Gusts

If there be a cloudy sky, with dark clouds driving fast under higher clouds, expect violent gusts of wind.

Red

Red clouds at sunrise foretell wind; at sunset, a fine day for the morrow. - Bacon.

Narrow, horizontal, red clouds after sunset in the west indicate rain before thirty-six hours.
Red clouds in the east, rain the next day.

Greenish

When you observe greenish tinted masses of composite cloud collect in the south-east and remain there for several hours, expect a succession of heavy rains and gales. - C. L. Prince.

After black clouds, clear weather.

Dark clouds in the west at sunrise indicate rain on
that day.

Clay-coloured and muddy clouds portend rain and
wind.
- Bacon.

Clouds before sunset of an amber or a gold colour,
and with gilt fringes, after the sun has sunk lower,
foretell fine weather.
- Bacon.

The wind-gale or prismatic colouring of the clouds
is considered by sailors a sign of rain.

Light, delicate, quiet tints or colours, with soft,
undefined forms of clouds, indicate and accompany
fine weather; but unusual or gaudy hues, with hard,
definitely outlined clouds, foretell rain, and probably
strong wind. - Fitzroy.

Black

Dull

Golden

Colouring

Brassy	Brassy-coloured clouds in the west at sunset indicate wind.
Dusky	Dusky or tarnished silver-coloured clouds indicate hail. - Howard.
Scud	Small, inky-looking clouds foretell rain; light scud clouds driving across heavy masses show wind and rain, but if alone may indicate wind only. - Fitzroy.
Bright and dark	If clouds be bright, 'Twill clear to-night; If clouds be dark, 'Twill rain - do you hark?
White	If the cloud be like in colour to a white skin, it is a sign of a storm. - Theophrastus ("Signs, etc." J. G. Wood's Translation).

Clouds above - water below.

He causeth the vapours to ascend from the ends of
the earth;
He maketh lightnings for the rain;
He bringeth the wind out of His treasuries.
- Psalm cxxxv. 7.

Generally squalls are preceded, or accompanied, or
followed by clouds; but the dangerous white squall of
the West Indies is indicated only by a rushing sound
and by white wave crests to windward.
- Fitzroy.

A squall cloud that one sees through or under is not
likely to bring or be accompanied by so much wind as
a dark, continued cloud extending beyond the horizon.
- Fitzroy.

If you see a cloud rise against the wind or side-wind,
when that cloud comes up to you, the wind will blow
the same way that the cloud came; and the same
rule holds good of a clear place when all the sky is
equally thick, except one clear edge.
- Shepherd of Banbury.

A small increasing white cloud about the size of a
hand to windward is a sure precursor of a storm.

A small, fast-growing black cloud in violent motion,
seen in the tropics, is called the "bull's eye", and
precedes the most terrible hurricanes.

Description of

Sometimes we see a cloud that's dragonish,
A vapour sometimes like a bear or lion,
A towered citadel, a pendent rock,
A forked mountain, a blue promontory
With trees upon't that nod unto the world
And mock our eyes with air.
That which is now a horse, even with a thought
The rack dislimns and makes it indistinct
As water is in water.
- Shakespeare (Antony and Cleopatra).

Clouds

Increasing	Behold, there ariseth a little cloud out of the sea, like a man's hand... Prepare thy chariot, and get thee down, that the rain stop thee not. And it came to pass that the heaven was black with clouds and wind, and there was a great rain. - 1 Kings xviii. 44, 45.
Bank	A bench (or bank) of clouds in the west means rain. - Surrey.
Broken	When small dark clouds (broken nimbi) appear against a patch of blue sky, there will be rain before sunset. - C. L. Prince.
CIRRUS Definition	Parallel, flexuous, or diverging fibres, extensible in any or all directions. - Howard. Common names: Curl Cloud, Mares' Tails, Goat's Hair, etc. - T. Forster.
Indicating change	After a long run of clear weather the appearance of light streaks of cirrus cloud at a great elevation is often the first sign of change. - Jenyns.
Indicating wind	Long parallel bands of clouds in the direction of the wind indicate steady high winds to come.

Feathery clouds, like palm branches or the "fleur de lis", denote immediate or coming showers.
- Bacon.

Showery

If cirrus clouds dissolve and appear to vanish, it is an indication of fine weather.

Fine weather

Rain If the cirrus clouds appear to windward, and change to cirro-stratus, it is a sign of rain.

Sheet cirrus Sheet cirrus occurs with southerly and westerly, but rarely with steady northerly or north-easterly, winds, unless a change to a westerly or southerly quarter is approaching. - Hon. F. A. R. Russell.

Rain In unsettled weather sheet cirrus precedes more wind or rain.

The longer the dry weather has lasted, the less is rain likely to follow the cloudiness of cirrus.

Murky A large formation of murky white cirrus may merely indicate a backing of wind to an easterly quarter.

Feathery If a shower be approaching from the west, it may be seen shooting forth white feathery rays from its upper edge, often very irregular and crooked.

Cirrus of a long, straight, feathery kind, with soft edges and outlines, or with soft, delicate colours at sunrise and sunset, is a sign of fine weather.

This cloud often indicates the approach of bad weather.

Curdled cirrus

The rapid movement of a cloud, something between cirrus and cirro-cumulus, in distinct dense bars, in a direction at right angles to the length of the bars, is, by itself, a certain sign of a gale of wind. If the bars are sharply defined and close together, the severer will be the storm. Sometimes these bars remind one of the form of a gridiron. The bands move transversely, and generally precede the storm by from twelve to forty-eight hours.
- Hon. F. A. R. Russell.

Bar or ribbed cirrus

Curly wisps and blown-back pieces are not a bad sign.

Curled

Tails downwards	When the tails are turned downwards, fair weather or slight showers often follow.
Definite	The harder and more distinct the outline, and the more frequently particular forms are repeated, the worse the result.
Fibrous	Long, hard, greasy-looking streaks, with rounded edges or knobs, whether crossed by fibres at right angles or not, are a sign of storms; but the storms may be at a distance.
	Cottony shreds, rounded and clear in outline, indicate dangerous disturbances.
Tufty	Regular, wavy tufts, with or without cross lines, are bad, especially if the tufts end, not in fibres, but in rounded knobs.
Regular	Feathery cirrus in thick patches at equal distances apart is a sign of storm; so is any appearance of definite waves of alternate sky and cloud; so is any regular repetition of the same form.
Undulating	Slightly undulating lines of cirrus occur in fine weather; but anything like a deeply indented outline precedes heavy rain or wind.
Twisted	Cirrus simply twisted or in zigzag lines of a fibrous character often appears in fine weather; and if not hard, or knotted, or clearly marked off from a serene sky, does not often precede any important change.

Detached patches of cirrus, like little masses of wool
or knotted feathers, in a clear sky, and of unusual
figure, moving at more than the average rate, precede
disturbances of great magnitude. The rays in straight
lines are a good sign.
- [The last ten rules are by the Hon. F. A. R. Russell.]

Continued wet weather is attended by horizontal
sheets of cirrus clouds, which subside quickly,
passing into the cirro-stratus.

Indicating wet

When cirri merge into cirri-strati, and when
cumuli increase towards evening and become lower,
expect wet weather.

Streaky clouds across the wind foreshow rain.
- Scotland.

If cirrus clouds form in fine weather with a falling
barometer, it is almost sure to rain. - Howard.

These clouds announce the east wind. If their under
surface is level, and their streaks pointing upwards, they
indicate rain; if downwards, wind and dry weather.
- Howard.

Rain and
wind

If the cirrus clouds get lower and denser to leeward,
it presages bad weather from the opposite quarter.

Bad weather

The cirrus clouds are the swiftest of all, moving at an
average speed of seventy-eight miles an hour.
- Clayton.

Speed

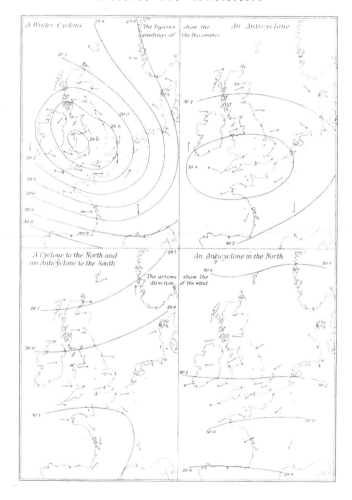

A Winter Cyclone

The figures show the readings of the Barometer

An Anticyclone

A Cyclone to the North and an Anticyclone to the South

The arrows show the direction of the wind

An Anticyclone in the North

RULES FOR WEATHER ACCORDING TO THE DIRECTION OF MOTION OF CIRRUS CLOUDS.

"Cirrus moving from north or north-east with a high barometer is a sign of settled weather in summer, and of temporarily fine weather in winter; with a low barometer, it is a sign of marked improvement in the weather.

Moving from east - a rare occurrence - is a sign of fine weather in winter, but of unsettled weather in summer. Cirrus moving from south-east (but it rarely does so with a low and unsteady barometer) is a sign of improving weather in winter, and in summer frequently indicates coming thunderstorms.

Moving from south generally indicates unsettled weather, especially in summer.

Moving from south-west indicates unsettled, and sometimes stormy, weather in winter. In summer it often precedes thunderstorms; but with a high barometric pressure and a high temperature it frequently has no disturbing influence, and is then usually replaced by cirro-macula (speckle cloud). Cirrus from west is commonly in summer a symptom of fair weather, but it is less so in winter.

Cirrus from north-west, when not tending to the form cirro-filum (thread-like cirrus), is an indication of temporary fine weather, especially in summer."
- Rev. Clement Ley (Cloudland).

V-POINT, OR POINT OF CONVEYANCE, FOR THE FIBRES OF CIRRO-FILUM (thread-like cirrus).

1. A V-point north commonly indicates improving weather over and to the south, but distant atmospheric disturbances in the north and north-west.

2. A V-point north-east, temporarily settled weather, especially with high barometer.

3. A V-point east, settled weather in winter; in summer, with high temperature, it sometimes indicates disturbances, which will be felt most to the south-west of the place of observation.

4. A V-point south-east, fine weather in winter, except when occurring immediately after heavy rain, when it is commonly followed by squalls. In summer it is almost invariably followed by thunder, with damp and sultry weather.

5. A V-point south with fairly low barometer, after a fall of rain, indicates showery weather in summer, and rough, squally weather in winter, with south-west or west winds, especially if the cloud velocity is great. With a high barometer, it indicates in summer thunderstorms from south-west, but in winter may be taken as a sign of favourable weather.

6. A V-point south-west, moderately fine weather.

7. A V-point west, fine weather in the warm months. The weather to the south and south-east of the observer is then usually dry and warm, but to the extreme north-west unsettled. In winter it is a symptom of unsettled weather.

8. A V-point north-west is bad; when it occurs just after a rise in the barometer, it indicates a sudden fall, with wind and rain. A V-point between west-north-west and north-west, especially with rapid cloud movement, is always followed by unsettled weather.

Cirro-macula (speckle-cloud) nearly always occurs in warm weather, when the atmosphere at the earth's surface has but little lateral motion.
- Rev. Clement Ley (Cloudland).

Speckle cloud

Storms	When the cirrus clouds appear at lower elevations than usual, and with a denser character, expect a storm from the opposite quarter to the clouds.
Pointing upwards	When streamers point upward, the clouds are falling, and rain is at hand; when streamers point downwards, the clouds are ascending, and drought is at hand.
Streaky	When after a clear frost long streaks of cirrus are seen with their ends bending towards each other as they recede from the zenith, and when they point to the north-east, a thaw and a south-west wind may be expected.
Barred	The barred or ribbed cirrus is considered by the Hon. F. A. R. Russell as good a danger-signal as that given by a falling barometer.
Weather-head cirrus	In Shetland the name of 'weather-head' is given to a band of cirrus passing through the zenith; and they say if it lies north-east to south-west, good weather comes; but if south-east to north-west, a gale is looked for.

After a drought or a spell of fine weather, when mares' tails are seen running across the sky, followed next day at about the same hour by alto-cumulus, then rain will follow within twelve hours.
- Col. H. M. Saunders, of Cheltenham.

If in fair weather a thin cloud appears stretched at length and feathery, the winter will not end yet.
- Theophrastus ("Signs, etc." J. G. Wood's Translation).

Horizontal or slightly inclined masses, attenuated towards a part or the whole of their circumference, bent downwards, or undulated, separate, or in groups, or consisting of small clouds having these characters. - Howard.

Cirro-stratus clouds, according to the observation of Mr. John Aitken, are always in a decaying or diminishing condition.
- Nature (June 18, 1896).

If clouds look as if scratched by a hen,
Get ready to reef your topsails then.
- Nautical.

Hen's scarts [scratchings] and filly tails
Make lofty ships carry low sails.

One of the surest signs of rain with which I am acquainted is that of the sky assuming an almost colourless appearance in the direction of the wind, especially if lines of dark or muddy cirro-strati lie above and about the horizon, and the milkiness gradually become muddy. - E. J. Lowe.

Hairy

Comoid cirri, or cirri in detached tufts, called "mares's tails," may be regarded as a sign of wind, which follows, often blowing from the quarter to which the fibrous tails have previously pointed. - T. Forster.

Trace in the sky the painter's brush,
Then winds around you soon will rush.

The cloud called "goat's hair" or the "gray mare's tail" forebodes wind.

The form of cloud popularly called "Noah's ark" is also called the "magnetic cirrus," and is said to consist of fine ice crystals, and to be accompanied by magnetic disturbances.

A long stripe of cloud, sometimes called a salmon, sometimes a Noah's ark, when it stretches east and west, is a sign of a storm; but when north and south, of fine weather.

This is called in the Yorkshire dales "Noaship," and the old Danes called it "Nolskeppet."
- Dr. J. C. Atkinson (Forty Years in a Moorland Parish).

"When looking in a westerly or easterly direction, if the centre of the bank of cirro-velum is to the right of the point from which the edge, or the cirro-filum outside the edge, is moving the probability of bad weather is not nearly so great as if this centre

was to the left of this point. But looking in a northerly or southerly direction, if the centre lies to the right of the direction of motion of the edge of the bank, the ensuing weather will be worse than if it lies to the left."
- Rev. Clement Ley ("Cloudland").

Cloud ship

In the Eifel district of the Lower Rhine they say, when the "cloud ship" turns its head to the south, rain will soon follow.

Wane cloud

When a plain sheet of the wane cloud is spread over a large surface at eventide, or when the sky gradually thickens with this cloud, a fall of steady rain is usually the consequence.
- T. Forster.

Direction

In low pressure areas the stripes lie parallel to the isobars (lines of equal barometric pressure), while in high pressure areas the stripes cross the isobars at right angles. - Hildebrandsson.

Gloomy

Continuous cirrostrati gathering into unbroken gloom, and also the cloud called "goat's hair," or the "gray mare's tail," presage wind.
- Scotland.

Indicating wind

When after a shower the cirrostrati open up at the zenith, leaving broken or ragged edges pointing upwards, and settle down gloomily and compactly on the horizon, wind will follow, and will last for some time. - Scotland.

The cirro-stratus precedes winds and rains, and the approach of foul weather may sometimes be inferred from its greater or less abundance, and the permanent character it puts on.

If clouds appear high in air in their white trains, wind, and probably rain, will follow.

When ash-coloured masses of cumulo-stratus and cirro-stratus cloud collect over the sea, extending in a line from south-east to south-west, expect rain, and probably wind, on the second day.
- C. L. Prince.

If long lines of cirrostrati extend along the horizon, and are slightly contracted in their centre, expect heavy rain the following day.
- C. L. Prince.

The cirro-stratus is doubtless the one alluded to by Polonius in "Hamlet" as "very like a whale."

The fish (hake) shaped cloud, if pointing east and west, indicates rain; if north and south, more fine weather.
- Bedfordshire.

North and south, the sign of drought;
East and west, the sign of blast.

With cirrus

Light, fleecy clouds in rapid motion, below compact, dark cirro-strati, foretell rain near at hand. - Scotland.

Indicating thunder
CIRRO-CUMULUS
Definition

The waved cirro-stratus indicates heat and thunder.

Small, well-defined, roundish masses increasing from below. - Howard.

The average speed of cirro-cumulus clouds is seventy-one miles an hour.
- Clayton.

Indicating wind
Rain

Commonly called "mackerel sky."

Mackerel sky and mares' tails
Make lofty ships carry low sails.

Change

A mackerel sky denotes fair weather for that day, but rain a day or two after.

Mackerel sky, mackerel sky,
Never long wet and never long dry.

Mackerel clouds in sky,
Expect more wet than dry.

Mackerel scales,
Furl your sails.

If small white clouds are seen to collect together,
their edges appearing rough, expect wind.

Before thunder, cirro-cumulus clouds often appear in
very dense and compact masses, in close contact.

Indicating
thunder

A curdly sky will not leave the earth long dry.

Curdled

When cirro-cumuli appear in winter, expect warm
and wet weather. When cirri threads are brushed back
from a southerly direction, expect rain and wind.

Direction

Small floating clouds over a bank of clouds,
sign of rain.

Small

Wandering

In summer we apprehend a future storm when we see little black, loose clouds lower than the rest, wandering to and fro when at sunrise we see several clouds gather in the west; and, on the other hand, if these clouds disperse, it speaks fair weather.
- Ozanam.

Scattered

Fleecy clouds scattered over the sky denote storms; but clouds which rest upon one another like scales or tiles portend dry and fine weather.
- Bacon.

Dappled

A sky dappled with light clouds of the cirro-cumulus form in the early morning generally leads to a fine and warm day.
- Jenyns.

Dappled sky is not for long.
- France.

If woolly fleeces spread the heavenly way,
Be sure no rain disturbs the summer day.

A blue and white sky,
Never four-and-twenty hours dry.
- Northamptonshire.

A dappled sky,
like a painted woman,
soon changes its face.
- France.

Small white clouds,
like a flock of sheep,
driving north-west,
indicate continued fine weather.

If clouds appear like a flock of sheep, and red in
colour, wind follows.

The Germans call the white, fleecy cirro-cumulus
clouds "heaven's lambs."

The cirro-cumulus, when accompanied by the cumulo-
stratus, is a sure indication of a coming storm.

Storm

There is an intermediate form of sad-coloured cloud between cirro-stratus and cirro-cumulus, and which resembles waves seemingly equi-distant from each other, which is a sure indication of thunder.
- Basil Woodd Smith.

Outlines

If soft and delicate in outline, it may be followed by a continuance of fine weather; but if dense, abundant, and associated with cirrus, it signifies electrical disturbance and change of wind, often resulting in thunderstorms in summer or gales in winter.

High

High cirro-cumulus commonly appears a few hours or days before thunderstorms. It generally moves with the prevailing surface wind. The harder and more definite the outline, the more unsettled the coming weather. In winter clearly marked, high cirro-cumulus is a sign of bad weather. If the cloud be continuous in long streaks, dense, and with rounded, knobby outlines, stormy weather follows generally within two or three days.

Soft

When cirro-cumulus is seen overhead, if the fleeces gently merge into each other, and the edges are soft and transparent, settled weather prevails; and if the middle part of the fleeces look shadowy, so much the better.

Slow

Cirro-cumulus at a great height and in large masses, moving slowly from north-east, is a sign of the continuance of the wind in that quarter.
- Hon. F. A. R. Russell.

Convex or conical heaps increasing upwards from a
horizontal base.
- Howard.

Cumulus clouds are called rainballs in Lancashire.

Pendulous cumuli are compared in the Vedic hymns
to the udders of the cows of Indra.

In India, if a cumulus cloud have a stratum of flat
cloud above it, a coming storm is indicated.

Sometimes the clouds appear to be piled in several
tiers or stories, one above the other (Gilbert,
"Phys". iv. 1, declares that he has sometimes seen
and observed five together), whereof the lowest are
always the blackest, though it sometimes appears
otherwise, as the whiter most attract the sight. Two
stories, if thick, portend instant rain (especially if the
lower one appear overcharged); many tiers denote a
three days' rain.
- Bacon.

Refreshing showers or heavier rains are near
When piled in fleecy heaps the clouds appear.
- Aratus (J. Lamb).

If a black cloud eclipse the solar ray,
And sudden night usurp the place of day.
(Indicating rain.)
- Aratus (J. Lamb).

Opening and closing	If clouds open and close, rain will continue.
Round-topped	A round-topped cloud, with flattened base, Carries rainfall in its face.
White	A white loaded cloud, called by the ancients a white tempest, is followed in summer by showers of very small hail, in winter by snow. - Bacon.
Wind	Cumulus clouds high up are said to show that south and south-west winds are near at hand; and stratified clouds low down, that east or north winds will prevail. - Scotland.
Tower-like indicating rain	Large irregular masses of cloud, "like rocks and towers," are indicative of showery weather. If the barometer be low, rain is all the more probable. - Jenyns.

When clouds appear like rocks and towers,
The earth's refreshed by frequent showers.

When mountains and cliffs in the clouds appear,
Some sudden and violent showers are near.

In the morning mountains,
In the evening fountains.
- Herbert.

When the clouds rise in terraces of white, soon will the country of the corn priests be pierced with the arrows of rain. - Zuñi Indians.

If during a storm, with the north wind blowing, a white under-light appear from the north, but on the south a cumulus cloud is extended opposite to it, it generally indicates a change to fair weather.
- Theophrastus ("Signs, etc." J. G. Wood's Translation).

Before rain these clouds augment in volume with great rapidity, sink to a lower elevation, and become fleecy and irregular in appearance, with their surfaces full of protuberances. They usually also remain stationary, or else sail against the surface wind previous to wet weather.

Augmenting

When the clouds bank up the contrary way to the wind, there will be rain.

Banking up

If on a fair day in winter a white bank of clouds arise in the south, expect snow.

Water-waggons	The rounded clouds called "water-waggons" which fly alone in the lower currents of wind forebode rain. - T. Forster.
Diminishing	When the cumulus clouds are smaller at sunset than they were at noon, expect fair weather.
Wet calm	The formation of cumulus clouds to leeward during a strong wind indicates the approach of a calm with rain.
Indicating hail, snow, or rain	If clouds are formed like fleeces, deep and dense, or thick and close towards the middle, the edges being very white, while the surrounding sky is bright and blue, they are of a frosty coldness, and will speedily fall in hail, snow, or rain.
Storm	And another storm brewing; I hear it sing i' the wind. Yond' same black cloud, yond' huge one, looks like a foul bumbard that would shed his liquor... Yond' same cloud cannot chuse but fall by pailfuls. - Shakespeare ("Tempest").
	The pocky* cloud or heavy cumulus, looking like festoons of drapery, forebodes a storm. - Scotland.
Thunder	In summer or harvest, when the wind has been south for two or three days, and it grows very hot, and you see clouds rise with great white tops like towers, as if one were upon the top of another, and joined together with black on the nether side, there will be thunder and rain suddenly. If two such clouds arise, one on

* Pock, a bag

either hand, it is time to make haste to shelter.
- Shepherd of Banbury.

When cumulus clouds become heaped up to leeward during a strong wind at sunset, thunder may be expected during the night.

Well-defined cumuli, forming a few hours after sunrise, increasing towards the middle of the day, and decreasing towards evening, are indicative of settled weather: if instead of subsiding in the evening and leaving the sky clear they keep increasing, they are indicative of wet. - Jenyns.

Changing

The cirro-stratus blended with the cumulus, and either appearing intermixed with the heaps of the latter, or superadding a widespread structure to its base.
- Howard.

CUMULO-
STRATUS
Definition

When large masses of cumulo-strati cloud collect simultaneously in the north-east and south-west, with the wind east, expect cold rain or snow in the course of a few hours. The wind will ultimately back to north.
- C. L. Prince.

Collecting

When at sea, if the cumulo-stratus clouds appear on the horizon, it is a sign that the weather is going to break up.

On horizon

If there be long points, tails, or feathers hanging from the thunder or rain clouds, five or six or more degrees above the horizon, with little wind in summer, thunder may be expected, but the storm will be of short duration.

Tails or feathers

Streak	A horizontal streak or band of clouds immediately in front of the mountains on the east side of Salt Lake Valley is an indication of rain within one or two days. When black clouds cover the western horizon, rain will follow soon, and extend to the eastward over the valley. - United States.
Striped	If long strips of clouds drive at a slow rate high in air, and gradually become larger, the sky having been previously clear, expect rain.
NIMBUS Definition	A rain cloud - a cloud or system of clouds from which rain is falling. It is a horizontal sheet over which the cirrus spreads, while the cumulus enters it laterally and from beneath. - Howard.
Prophet clouds	When scattered patches or streaks of nimbus come driving up from the south-west, they are called by the sailors "prophet clouds," and indicate wind.
Bells	Hark! from the little village below us, the bells of the church are ringing for rain! Priests and peasants in long procession come forth and kneel on the arid plain. They have not long to wait, for I see in the south uprising a little cloud, That before the sun shall be set will cover the sky above us as with a shroud. - Longfellow ("Golden Legend").
Storm	If a little cloud suddenly appear in a clear sky, especially if it come from the west, or somewhere in the south, there is a storm brewing. - Bacon.

Clouds

See we not hanging in the clouds each hour
So many seas, still threat'ning down to pour,
Supported only by th' aire's agitation,
Selfly too weak for the least weight's foundation.
- Du Bartas ("Divine Weekes").

STRATUS Definition	A widely extended, continuous, horizontal sheet, increasing from below. - Howard.
Fine	These clouds have always been regarded as the harbingers of fine weather, and there are few finer days in the year than when the morning breaks out through a disappearing stratus cloud.
Night	A stratus at night, with a generally diffused fog the next morning, is usually followed by a fine day, if the barometer be high and steady. If the barometer keep rising, the fog may last all day; if the barometer be low, the fog will probably turn to rain. - Jenyns.

When mountains extend north and south, if fog or mist comes from the west, expect fair weather.
If mist comes from the top of mountains, expect rain in summer, snow in winter.
- Apache Indians.

Thin, white, fleecy, broken mist, slowly ascending the sides of a mountain whose top is uncovered, predicts a fair day.
- Scotland.

A few parallel streaks of cloud, seldom more than three or four in number, appearing either as white streaks on the blue or, more rarely, as darker streaks against nimbus or cumulo-nimbus, are a sure prognostic of thunder.
- B. Woodd Smith ("Nature", June 18, 1896).

This is no pilgrim's morning - yon grey mist lies
upon hill and dale and field and forest.
- Sir W. Scott ("Pirate").

Storm

Oh! The morning mist lies heavy upon yonder
chain of isles, nor has it permitted us since daybreak
even a single glimpse of Fitful Head.
(Indicating approaching storm.)
- Sir W. Scott ("Pirate", ch. iv.).

On hills

If mist rise to the hilltops and there stay,
expect rain shortly.

When the mist comes from the hill,
Then good weather it doth spill;
When the mist comes from the sea.
Then good weather it will be.
When the mist creeps up the hill,
Fisher, out and try your skill;
When the mist begins to nod,
Fisher, then put past your rod.
- Kirkcudbright.

Rising and
falling

Misty clouds, forming or hanging on heights,
show wind and rain coming, if they remain,
increase, or descend. If they rise or disperse,
the weather will improve.
- Fitzroy.

Clouds upon hills, if rising,
do not bring rain;
if falling, rain follows.

Clouds

Thick   When the clouds on the hilltops are thick and in motion, rain to the south-west is regarded as certain to follow. - Scotland.

Small   When it gangs up i' fops,*
It'll fa' down i' drops.
- North Country.

Hanging   When mountains and hills appear capped by clouds that hang about and embrace them, storms are imminent. - Bacon.

Ascending   When the clouds go up the hill,
They'll send down water to turn a mill.
- Hampshire.

Hymettus   If during the winter there is a long cloud over Hymettus, it indicates a prolongation of the winter.

64   * Small clouds on hills.

Athos, Olympus and the peaks of mountains
generally, if covered by cloud, indicate a storm.
- Theophrastus ("Signs, etc." J. G. Wood's Translation).

When Olympus, Athos, and generally all hills
that give indications, have their tops clear, it
indicates fair weather.
- Theophrastus ("Signs, etc." J. G. Wood's Translation).

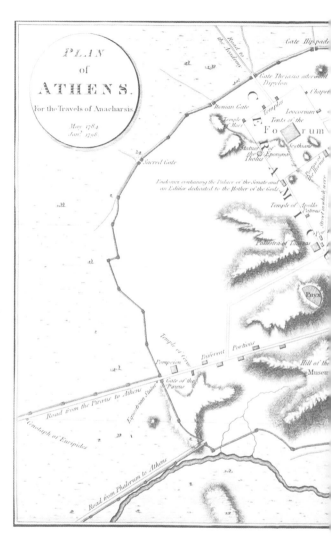

PLAN

of

ATHENS.

For the Travels of Anacharsis.

May 1784.
Jan.ʸ 1798.

Road to the Academy

Gate Hippade

Gate Thriasia otherwise
Dipylon

Chapel

Roman Gate

Temples

Leocorium

Temple of Mars

Tents of the

Fo rum

Statue of Scythian
the Eponymi
Tholus

Sacred Gate

Enclosure containing the Palace of the Senate and
an Edifice dedicated to the Mother of the Gods.

Temple of Apollo
Patrous

Palaestra of Taureas

Pnyx

Temple of Ceres

Different Portices

Pompeion

Hill of the
Museum

Gate of the
Pirceus

Road from the Piraeus to Athens

Equestrian Statue

Cenotaph of Euripides

Road from Phalerum to Athens

MOUNT ANCHESMUS

Gate of Melite

Street leading to Gate

House of Phœnix

LITE

na Aristobuli Aristocles

Gate Diomeia

Gymnasium

Temple and Gardens of Venus

Chapel of Æsculap.

Prytaneum

Street to the West

CITADEL

Temple of Minerva

Theatre of Bacchus

Ancient Temple of Bacchus or the Marshes

MNÆ

the Marshes

Temple to Jupiter

Gate of Ænens

Odeum

Gymnasium

DROMOS

Altar of Python

Temple of Diana Agrotera

Temple of Ceres

AGRÆ

MOUNT

HYMETTUS

ILISSUS R.

English Yards

Olympian Stadia

French Toises

If the lesser Hymettus (which is called Dry) has a small cloud in its hollow, it is a sign of rain; and if the Great Hymettus in summer has white clouds above and on its side it is a sign of rain.

So also if Dry Hymettus has white clouds above and on its side.

[The Hymettus (Greater and Less) Hills, about five miles Southeast of Athens.]
- Theophrastus ("Signs, etc." J. G. Woods Translation).

Whenever a long white cloud envelops Hymettus downwards from its peaks at night, rain occurs, as a rule, within a few days.
- Theophrastus ("Signs, etc." J. G. Wood's Translation).

See, Glaucus! The deep sea already is surging with waves; and around the tops of the hills an upright cloud stands encircling them-the sign of a storm.
- Archilochus (quoted by Theophrastus: "Signs, etc." J. G. Wood's Translation).

In whatever direction a cloud stretches out from the peak of a mountain, in that direction will the wind blow.
- Theophrastus ("Signs, etc." J. G. Wood's Translation).

Whenever the clouds girt the mountains quite down to the sea, it is a sign of fair weather.
- Theophrastus ("Signs, etc." J. G. Wood's Translation).

If clouds settle down on the back of a mountain, the wind will blow from behind it also.
- Theophrastus ("Signs, etc." J. G. Wood's Translation).

When the Pendle's Head is free from clouds, Pendle's Head
the people thereabout expect a halcyon day,
and those on the banks of the Can (or Kent) in
Westmoreland can tell what weather to look for
from the voice of its falls.

For when they to the north the noise do easiest hear,
They constantly aver the weather will be clear.
And when they to the south, again they boldly say
It will be clouds or rain the next approaching day.
- Drayton ("Polyolbion").

When the South Downs look blue and near after   South Downs
heavy rain, a gale may be expected within thirty
hours. When on a cloudless summer day you
perceive a white flocculent mist lying upon the
summit of the South Downs (i.e. from Mount
Harry to Lewes Racecourse), expect very hot
weather within three days. - C. L. Prince.

Bell Rock

Clouds on Bell Rock Light
mean rain at Arbroath.

Firle Head

When Firle Hill and Long Man has a cap,
We at A'ston gets a drap. - Sussex.

Wolsonbury

When Wolsonbury has a cap,
Hurstpierpoint will have a drap.
- Sussex.

Ross

Clouds on Ross-shire Hills mean rain at Ardersier,
on the south-east of the Moray Frith.

Cocking

A curious phenomenon is observable in the
neighbourhood of Cocking, West Sussex.
From the leafy recesses of the hangers of beech on
the escarpments of the downs, there rises in unsettled
weather a mist which rolls among the trees like the
smoke out of a chimney. This exhalation is called

"foxes-brewings," whatever that may mean, and if it tends westward towards Cocking, rain follows speedily. Hence the local proverb:

> "When Foxes-brewings go to Cocking,
> Foxes-brewings come back dropping."
> - Lower ("History of Sussex").

Clouds on Orkney Isles
mean rain at Cape Wrath.

Clouds on Kilpatrick Hills mean rain at
Eaglesham, in Renfrewshire.

Clouds on Ailsa Craig mean rain at Cumbrae.

Sailors say it is a sign of bad weather when the
"tablecloth" (a cloud so called) is spread on
Table Mountain.

Clouds

Bever

If Bever hath a cap,
You churls of the vale look to that.
- Leicestershire.

Ladie Lift

When Ladie Lift*
Puts on her shift,
She feares a downright raine;
But when she doffs it, you will finde
The raine is o'er, and still the winde,
And Phœbus shine againe. - Herefordshire.

Skiddaw

If Skiddaw hath a hat,
Scruffel wots full well of that. - Cumberland.

When Skiddaw hath a cap,
Criffel wots fu' well of that.
Heavy clouds on Skiddaw, especially with a south
wind, the farmer of Kirkpatrick Fleming looks on as
an indication of coming rain.
[Note. - Skiddaw lies to the south of the place.]

* A clump of trees near Weobley

When Moncayo and Guara have their white caps on,
It is good for Castile and better for Aragon. - Spain.

Moncayo

When Traprain puts on his hat,
The Lothian lads may look to that.
- Haddingtonshire.

Traprain

When Ruberslaw puts on his cowl,
The Dunion on his hood,
Then a' the wives of Teviotside
Ken there will be a flood.
- Roxburghshire.

Ruberslaw

[Also said of Craigowl and Collie Law in
Forfarshire, substituting "Lundy lads" for "the
wives of Teviotside." - Robert Chambers.]

Craigowl and
Collie Law

When Falkland Hill puts on his cap,
The Howe o' Fife will get a drap;
And when the Bishop draws his cowl,
Lookout for wind and weather foul.

Falkland
Hill,
Lomond
Range

When Cheviot ye see put on his cap,
Of rain ye'll have a wee bit drap.
- Scotland.

Cheviot

When Largo Law puts on his hat,
Let Kellie Law beware of that;
When Kellie Law gets on his cap,
Largo Law may laugh at that.
- Scotland.
[Note. - Largo Law is to the south-west of Kellie Law.]

Largo Law

Scotch Hills

A cloud on Sidlaw Hills foretells rain to Carmylie.
A cloud on Bin Hill foretells rain to Cullen.
A cloud on Paps of Jura foretells rain to Gigha.
A cloud on Mull of Kintyre foretells rain to Cara.

Cairnsmore

When Cairnsmore wears a hat,
The Macher's Rills may laugh at that.
[Note. - Cairnsmore is north-north-east of Macher's Rills,
Wigtownshire, Scotland.]

When Cairnsmuir puts on his hat,
Palmuir and Skyreburn laugh at that.
[Note. - Palmuir and Skyreburn are rivulets which rise
rapidly whenever rain falls about Cairnsmuir.]

When Criffel wears a hat
Skiddaw wots full we o' that.

Criffel

If Corsancone put on his cap, and the Knipe be
clear, it will rain within twenty-four hours.
[Note. - This is a sign which it is said never fails. Corsancone
Hill is to the East and the Knipe to the south-west of the New
Cumnock districts, where the proverb is current.]

Corsancone

The rolling of clouds landward and their gathering
about the summit of Criffel is regarded as a sign of
foul weather in Dumfries and Kirkpatrick Fleming,
and intervening parishes.
[Note. - Criffel is to the Southwest of the place.]

Criffel

Clouds

Craighill

There is a high wooded hill above Lochnaw Castle;
Take care when Lady Craighill puts on her mantle.
The Lady looks high and knows what is coming;
Delay not one moment to get under covering.
[Note. - The hill lies to the north-west of the district where this
doggerel is quoted.]

Riving Pike

If Riving Pike do wear a hood,
Be sure the day will ne'er be good.
- Lancashire.

Helm cloud

A cloud, called the "helm cloud," or "helm bar,"
hovering about the hilltops for a day or two, is said
to presage wind and rain. - Yorkshire.

Clouds

Lookout

When Lookout Mountain has its cap on,
it will rain in six hours. - United States

Mists

Spring

If mists occur after the vernal equinox, they indicate airs and winds till the sixth month thereafter.
- Theophrastus ("Signs, etc." J. G. Wood's Translation).

Disappearing

If mists and fogs ascend and return upwards, they denote rain; and if this take place suddenly, so that they appear to be sucked up, they foretell winds; but if they fall and rest in the valleys, it will be fine weather.
- Bacon.

Vapours and winds

Wherever there is a plentiful generation of vapours, and that at certain times, you may be sure that at those times periodical winds will arise.
- Bacon.

White

White mist in winter indicates frost.
- Scotland.

Black

Black mist indicates coming rain.

Mist and rain

Mists above, water below.
- Spain.

In low ground

If mists rise in low ground and soon vanish, expect fair weather.
- Shepherd of Banbury.

A white mist in the evening, over a meadow with a river, will be drawn up by the sun next morning, and the day will be bright. Five or six fogs successively drawn up portend rain.

River

Where there are high hills, and the mist which hangs over the lower lands draws towards the hills in the morning, and rolls up to the top, it will be fair; but if the mist hangs upon the hills, and drags along the woods, there will be rain.
- Rev. W. Jones.

Rising

In the evenings of autumn and spring, vapour arising from a river is regarded as a sure indication of coming frost. - Scotland.

A northern harr (mist)
Brings weather from far.

Northern

Mists dispersing on the plain
Scatter away the clouds and rain;
But when they rise to the mountain-tops,
They'll soon descend in copious drops.

Spreading

Three foggy or misty mornings indicate rain.
- Oregon.

Misty morning

Mists

Haze

Haze and western sky purple indicate fair weather.

Hazy weather is thought to prognosticate frost in
winter, snow in spring, fair weather in summer,
and rain in autumn.
- Scotland.

A sudden haze coming over the atmosphere is due
to the mixing of two currents of unequal temperatures:
it may end in rain, or in an increase of temperature;
or it may be the precursor of a change, though not
immediate. - Jenyns.

Dew

The dews of the evening industriously shun;
They're the tears of the sky for the loss of the sun.

Evening

If the dew lies plentifully on the grass after a fair
day, it is a sign of another.

If not, and there is no wind, rain must follow.
- Rev. W. Jones.

When in the morning the dew is heavy and remains
long on the grass, when the fog in the valleys is slowly
dispersed and lingers on the hillsides, when the clouds
seem to be taking a higher place, and when a few loose
cirro-strati float gently along, serene weather may be
expected for the greater part of that day.
- Scotland.

Dew and fog

If in clear summer nights there is no dew, expect rain
next day.
- C. L. Prince.

Night

Dew is an indication of fine weather; so is fog.
- Fitzroy.

Fine weather

Dew is produced in serene weather and in calm places.
- Aristotle.

Calm

Dew

Dispersing	If the dew is evaporated immediately upon the sun rising, rain and storm follow in the afternoon; but if it stays and glitters for a long time after sunrise, the day continues fair. De Quincey's "Note to Analects from Richter."
Profuse	If there is a profuse dew in summer, it is about seven to one that the weather will be fine. - E. J. Lowe.
Evening	With dew before midnight, The next day will sure be bright.
South wind	During summer a heavy dew is sometimes followed by a southerly wind in the afternoon.
Heavy	If there is a heavy dew, it indicates fair weather; no dew, it indicates rain.
Rain	If nights three dewless there be, 'Twill rain you're sure to see.
Mountain	When the dew is seen shining on the leaves, the mist rolled down from the mountain last night. - Zuñi Indians.
No dew	When there is no dew at such times as usually there is, it foreshoweth rain. - Wing, 1649.

Fog

Falling   When the fog falls, fair weather follows; when it rises, rain ensues.

August   In the Mississippi valley, when fogs occur in August, expect fever and ague in the following fall.

Damp   If there be a damp fog or mist, accompanied by wind, expect rain.

Light   Light fog passing under sun from south to north in the morning indicates rain in twenty-four or forty-eight hours.

With frost   If there be continued fog, expect frost.
- United States.

When the fog goes up the mountain, you may go hunting; when it comes down the mountain, you may go fishing. In the former case it will be fair, in the latter it will rain.

Fog

Change   Fogs are signs of a change.

Winter   Heavy fog in winter, when it hangs below trees, is
              followed by rain.

Sea and   A fog from the sea
hills   Brings honey to the bee;
              A fog from the hills
              Brings corn to the mills.
              - Pembrokeshire.

Fog from seaward, fair weather; Sea
fog from landward, rain.
- New England.

When with hanging fog smoke rises vertically, Hanging
rain follows.

Whenever there is a fog, there is little or no rain.
- Theophrastus ("Signs, etc." J. G. Wood's Translation).

Fog is caused by a white bear Superstition
drinking too much water and bursting.
During fog, bears come out.
- Labrador.

Rain

When God wills, it rains with any wind. - Spain.   Wind

Some rain, some rest;
Fine weather isn't always best.

No one so surely pays his debt   Changes
As wet to dry and dry to wet.
- Wiltshire.

Rain, rain pouring   Pouring
Sets the bulls a-roaring. - Suffolk.

With the rain of the north-east comes the ice fruit [hail].   North-east
- Zuñi Indians.

Rain from the north-east in Germany continues
three days.

Rain from the east,   East
Two days at least.

Rain from the south prevents the drought;   South
But rain from the west is always best.

Rain which sets in with a south wind on the north
Pacific coast will probably last.

If it begin to rain from the south, with a high wind, for two or three hours, and the wind falls, but the rain continues, it is likely to rain twelve hours or more, and does usually rain till a north wind clears the air. These long rains seldom hold above twelve hours, or happen above once a year.
- Shepherd of Banbury.

Rain with south or south-west thunder brings squalls on successive days.

West

When rain comes from the west, it will not last long.
- United States.

Short

The faster the rain, the quicker the hold up.
- Norfolk.

Long foretold

Rain long foretold, long last;
Short notice, soon past.

Mountains

Rain comes from a mass of vapour which is cooled.
- Aristotle.

Mountains cool the uplifted vapour, converting it again into water.
- Aristotle.

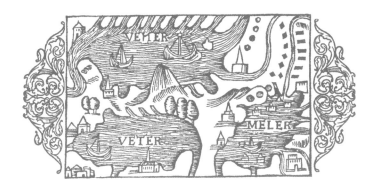

Small showers last long,
but sudden storms are short.
- Shakespeare ("Richard II").

Rain before seven,
Lift before eleven.

If rain begins at early morning light,
'Twill end ere day at noon is bright.

Morning rains are soon past.
- France.

Rain afore church
Rain all the week, little or much.
- Norfolk.

Night rains
Make drowned fens.
- East Anglia.

Custom	In Burmah the inhabitants have a custom of pulling a rope to produce rain. A rain party and a drought party tug against each other, the rain party being allowed the victory, which in the popular notion is generally followed by rain. - Folk-Lore Journal, vol. i. p. 214.
Night and morning	When it rains in the morning, it will be fine at night. - China.
Before sunrise	If it begin to rain an hour or two before sunrising, it is likely to be fair before noon, and so continue that day; but if the rain begin an hour after sunrising, it is likely to rain all that day, except the rainbow be seen before it rains. - Shepherd of Banbury.

When it rains about the break of day,
The traveller's sorrows pass away.
- China.

If the rain falls on the dew, it will fall all day.
- Bergamo.

A fall of small drizzling rain, especially in the
morning, is a sure sign of wind to follow.
- Newhaven.

If it rain at midnight with a south wind, it will
generally last above twelve hours.

After rains, the wind most often blows in the places
where the rain falls, and winds often cease when rain
begins to fall.
- Aristotle.

Rain

Five days' rain, ten days' wind, are both good omens.
- China.

A hasty shower of rain falling when the wind has raged some hours, soon allays it.
- Pointer.

Small rain abates high wind.
- France.

Marry the rain to the wind, and you have a calm.

Small

A small rain may allay a great storm.
- T. Fuller.

Sudden

Sudden rains never last long; but when the air grows thick by degrees, and the sun, moon, and stars shine dimmer and dimmer, then it is likely to rain six hours usually.
- Shepherd of Banbury.

From north or south

It is better both for plants and animals that rain from the north should precede that from the south, but it should be sweet and not salt to the taste.
- Theophrastus ("Signs, etc." J. G. Wood's Translation).

Sunshine

If it rains when the sun shines, it will rain the next day.

If it rains while the sun is shining,
the devil is beating his grandmother.
He is laughing, and she is crying.

After rain comes sunshine.

Sunshine and shower, rain again to-morrow.

If it rain when the sun shines, it will surely rain the next day about the same hour. - Suffolk.

A sunshiny shower
Never lasts half an hour. - Bedfordshire.

Bright rain
Makes fools fain [glad]. - Scotland.

If short showers come during dry weather, they are said to "harden the drought" and indicate no change. - Scotland.

Showers short

There is usually fair weather before a settled course of rain. - Fitzroy.

Preceded by fair weather

A foot deep of rain
Will kill hay and grain;
But three feet of snow
Will make them come mo [more]. - Devonshire.

Rain and snow

If hail appear after a long course of rain,
it is a sign of clearing up. - Scotland.

Followed by hail

Wet continues if the ground dries up too soon.

Drying

Who soweth in rain, he shall reap it with tears. - Tusser.

Sowing

Though it rains, do not neglect to water. - Spain.

Watering

After great droughts come great rains. - Holland.

Drought

When the rain causes bubbles to rise in water it falls upon, the shower will last long.

Causing bubbles

The first and last rains bring the ague. - Spain.

Ague

Rainbows

The old Norsemen called the rainbow
"The bridge of the gods."
- C. Swainson.

A rainbow can only occur when the clouds
containing or depositing the rain are opposite to the
sun; and in the evening the rainbow is in the east,
and in the morning in the west; and as our heavy
rains in this climate are usually brought by the
westerly wind, a rainbow in the west indicates that
the bad weather is on the road, whereas the rainbow
in the east proves that the rain in these clouds is
passing from us.
- Sir Humphry Davy (in "Salmonia").

East and west

When a rainbow is formed in an approaching cloud,
expect a shower; but when in a receding cloud,
fine weather.
- C. L. Prince.

In cloud

A rainbow in spring indicates fair weather
for twenty-four hours.

In spring

When a rainbow appears in wind's eye,
rain is sure to follow.

In wind's eye

A dog in the morning,
Sailor, take warning;
A dog in the night
Is the sailor's delight.
[A sun-dog, in nautical language, is a small rainbow
near the horizon. - Roper.]

Rainbows

Windward   Rainbow to windward, foul fall the day;
            Rainbow to leeward, damp runs away.
            - Nautical.

Fair and foul   If a rainbow appear in fair weather, foul will
                 follow; but if a rainbow appear in foul weather,
                 fair will follow.

Broken   Whenever you observe the rainbow to be broken in
          two or three places, or perhaps only half of it visible,
          expect rainy weather for two or three days.
          - C. L. Prince.

Rainbow in morning shows that shower is west
of us, and that we shall probably get it. Rainbow
in the evening shows that shower is east of us,
and is passing off.
- United States.

A rainbow in the morn, put your hook in the corn;
A rainbow in the eve, put your hook in the sheave.
- Cornwall.